Allegiances

Books by William Stafford

Allegiances

The Rescued Year

Traveling through the Dark

West of Your City

Allegiances

by William Stafford

1817

HARPER & ROW, PUBLISHERS
New York, Evanston, and London

"Remembering Althea," "Montana Eclogue," "Vacation Trip," and "So Long" (originally entitled "At the Level of Love") appeared originally in *The New Yorker*

"Monuments for a Friendly Girl at a Tenth Grade Party," "Reaching Out to Turn On a Light," "In Sublette's Barn," "The Girl Engaged to the Boy Who Died," "Return to Single-Shot," "What I Heard Whispered at the Edge of Liberal, Kansas," "In Fur," "How I Escaped," and "In Fog" appeared originally in *Poetry*

"Holcomb, Kansas" appeared originally in *New American Review #4*

"Allegiances" appeared originally in *The Southern Review*

Other poems appearing in this volume were originally published in *The Critical Quarterly, Sponsa Regis, The Carleton Miscellany, Poetry Australia, The Hudson Review, The Kenyon Review, The Little Review, Writer's Digest, The Atlantic Monthly, The Poetry Bag, Poetry Northwest, World Order, Harper's Magazine, The Nation, The North American Review, The Oregon Centennial Anthology, Cloud Marauder, The Distinctive Voice, Talisman, Aperture, The Colorado State Review, The Saturday Review, Book Week, The Colorado Quarterly, The Virginia Quarterly,* and *The Denver Quarterly*

LIBRARY OF CONGRESS CATALOG CARD NUMBER: 73-95986

Contents

III

This Book

Late, at the beginning of cold,
you push your breath toward home.
Silence waits at the door.
You stamp, go in, start the fire—
from any part of the room I suddenly say,
"Hello," but do not get in your way.

Quiet as all books, I wait, and promise
we'll watch the night: you turn a page;
winter misses a stride. You see
the reason for time, for everything in the sky.
And into your eyes I climb, on the strongest
thread in the world, weaving the dark and the cold.

With Kit, Age 7, at the Beach

We would climb the highest dune,
from there to gaze and come down:
the ocean was performing;
we contributed our climb.

Waves leapfrogged and came
straight out of the storm.
What should our gaze mean?
Kit waited for me to decide.

Standing on such a hill,
what would you tell your child?
That was an absolute vista.
Those waves raced far, and cold.

"How far could you swim, Daddy,
in such a storm?"
"As far as was needed," I said,
and as I talked, I swam.

Bess

Ours are the streets where Bess first met her
cancer. She went to work every day past the
secure houses. At her job in the library
she arranged better and better flowers, and when
students asked for books her hand went out
to help. In the last year of her life
she had to keep her friends from knowing
how happy they were. She listened while they
complained about food or work or the weather.
And the great national events danced
their grotesque, fake importance. Always

Pain moved where she moved. She walked
ahead; it came. She hid; it found her.
No one ever served another so truly;
no enemy ever meant so strong a hate.
It was almost as if there was no room
left for her on earth. But she remembered
where joy used to live. She straightened its flowers;
she did not weep when she passed its houses;
and when finally she pulled into a tiny corner
and slipped from pain, her hand opened
again, and the streets opened, and she wished all well.

4

Monuments for a Friendly Girl
at a Tenth Grade Party

The only relics left are those long
spangled seconds our school clock chipped out
when you crossed the social hall
and we found each other alive,
by our glances never to accept our town's
ways, torture for advancement,
nor ever again be prisoners by choice.

Now I learn you died
serving among the natives of Garden City,
Kansas, part of a Peace Corps
before governments thought of it.

Ruth, over the horizon your friends eat
foreign chaff and have addresses like titles,
but for you the crows and hawks patrol
the old river. May they never
forsake you, nor you need monuments
other than this I make, and the one
I hear clocks chip in that world we found.

Holcomb, Kansas

The city man got dust on his shoes and carried
a box of dirt back to his apartment.
He joined the killers in jail and saw things
their way. He visited the scene of the crime
and backed people against the wall with his typewriter
and watched them squirm. He saw how it was.
And they—they saw how it was: he was
a young man who had wandered onto the farm
and begun to badger the homefolk.
So they told him stories for weeks while he
fermented the facts in his little notebook.

Now the wide country has gone sober again.
The river talks all through the night, proving
its gravel. The valley climbs back into its hammock
below the mountains and becomes again only what
it is: night lights on farms make little blue domes
above them, bright pools for the stars; again
people can visit each other, talk easily,
deal with real killers only when they come.

A Gesture Toward an Unfound Renaissance

There was the slow girl in art class,
less able to say where our lessons led: we
learned so fast she could not follow us.
But at the door each day I looked back
at her rich distress, knowing almost enough
to find a better art inside the lesson.

And then, late at night, when the whole town
was alone, the current below the rumbly bridge
at Main Street would go an extra swirl
and gurgle, once, by the pilings;
and at my desk at home, or when our house
opened above my bed toward the stars,
I would hear that one intended lonely sound,
the signature of the day, the ratchet of time
taking me a step toward here, now, and this
look back through the door that always closes.

Remembering Althea

When you came out of your house
and put your hand on the August day,
walls of the barn delicate in the light
began the season that would ribbon away
all that we saw and blow it past the world,

For after we contended at school, we had
our war, sought outward for enemies, awarded
each other greatness; and you were left
forgotten awhile: why touch what was
already ours, when there was more—cities, glory?

For you held no power, Althea,
according to any of us; but after the others
asserted, claimed their place, posed for
every storm, your true beam found all. That
August day is yours, and every honor

You gave away. I remember Jeff,
who always won, and Ben, and his sister,
that whole class: they are only your chorus,
because you waved and it was far and the end,
you knew, delicately, through amber, that August day.

Reaching Out to Turn on a Light

Every lamp that approves its foot
shyly reminds of how Ellen stood.

Every bowl, every shadow that leans forth,
hunts vaguely for the pattern by her door.

One summer, I remember, a giant beautiful cloud
stood beyond the hill where Ellen lived.

It has been years, and we hardly looked back;
now, except for times like this, we hardly ever look.

There may be losses too great to understand
that rove after you and—faint and terrible—
    rip unknown through your hand.

The Last Day

To Geronimo rocks were the truth,
water less, air not at all;
but the opposite he had to learn:
his hollow hand, his nothing breath—
they filled the world when all his loss
was a place to hide. These cliffs
where he lived, those miles of stone—
relief came when they drifted across
his lightest thought; and he bought
his life in those dead hills
by the way they leaned as he touched
their sides and loved the air.

Then he could fall.

At the Grave of My Brother

The mirror cared less and less at the last, but
the tone of his voice roamed, had more to find,
back to the year he was born; and the world
that saw him awhile again went blind.

Drawn backward along the street, he disappeared
by the cedars that faded a long time ago
near the grave where Mother's hair was a screen
but she was crying. I see a sparrow

Chubby like him, full of promise, barely
holding a branch and ready to fly.
In his house today his children begin
to recede from this year and go their own way.

Brother: Good-bye.

Father's Voice

"No need to get home early;
the car can see in the dark."
    He wanted me to be rich
    the only way we could,
    easy with what we had.

And always that was his gift,
given for me ever since,
    easy gift, a wind
    that keeps on blowing for flowers
    or birds wherever I look.

World, I am your slow guest,
one of the common things
    that move in the sun and have
    close, reliable friends
    in the earth, in the air, in the rock.

Observation Car and Cigar

Tranquility as his breath, his eye a camera
that believes, he follows rails that only last
one trip, then vanish. (Suppose America
tried and then was the West once more, but this time
no one found it? He has felt that much
alone.) Remembering with smoke, he uses
the haze as authentic (the authentic loves not kept
for display fade authentically and become
priceless, never to be exchanged). A silver
evening light follows the train silently
over a great bridge. Like a camera that
believes, he follows an arch into faded
authentic scenes that bring something presented again
and yet all new: traveling, our loves are brought
before us and followed securely into a new evening.

In Sublette's Barn

Sublette moved up the Cimarron alert
all day for hostiles; he feared what he was finding:
no one had reported this place; once you made
camp it was time to move—it soon felt old.
He had always been the kind of man who had
the kind of horses that would turn
to look at you. In talk he listened to the current,
not the words. Now, he heard something in the country.
Maybe he had listened too long.

His friends had scattered, far valleys, not anywhere
the right place—how could it be?—or the wrong either:
Scatter. But for him the earth had lent itself, was
always his. Steady now, he still did not start any bluff moves:
what would happen was what he would intend, though the
world
would swerve sometime, and his hand would miss the handle.
By his campfire, his own tea—warm or cool—was what he would
deserve. He carried an extra cup.

II

But he was lost a new way that winter, began to find
tracks he could read better and better, till all
he found went out and intensified the valley:
he came around the Cimarron breaks into a land that
began to tense itself all day for deliberate snow.
He camped there well but was afraid: once that place
was found, the West had come; no one could undiscover it.
Like a badger by that stream—so strong the trap that

grabbed his feet was bent, with his teeth grooved on everything
he bit, and miles ringed all around, so target was the place,
where—now—the sky kept saying out and out because
its color would never be at all but what it was—he took
his paw back from the steel, and watched the trap.

III

The river stopped, for him; the clouds were holding
there: Sublette's big valley crossed by trails that
surfaced under a round reminder of gold or copper sun,
shimmered toward him. He looked across a place the air
filled—saved only by his weakness, forms of monotony,
   meanings
that made the world regular enough to offer choices.
He had not stopped until the West climbed in at him;
but now it was the last available ranch, a place that still
   says:

     You never told a friend, even, a lie. You
     never tried for the good feeling you get from over-
       valuing
     something that's yours—indulgence that seems austere.
     It is not. You were the one who always began on the
       level part,
     forth on a line trued for accepted real things,
     looking across the prairies a rod of steady light.

Held where the sky touched land along the edge,
his trail encountered all his eye grooved, and went on.
Reluctant hero, he had let one deed at a time take him;
then where he was, was everywhere: the kind of trip he
took turned into carving; the knifeblade led, the hand
reluctant but so steady it was always at the place

it should be and with force as if the earth turned
for his body and the light held back until his eyes
met it, all equal, all come right at once.
His fate was righteousness.

That was his land, but no one there to know. By
following him we blunder into it. Here now, fall or winter,
anytime, it's here. You move your hand across
till the fingers frame a certain line trees make by the
river always there: that's the way the man Sublette became.
Reluctantly he found and kept on finding himself the man
the land meant. It subsided and became a state.

Now snow terms are imposed for us; the wind climbs
around the barn. Eyes level—rafter, higher, window
defense above the storm—we climb, years of soft dust
molded—rafter, stanchions, haymow. No one can sound
the deep rope to those days, hold level the wide ranch
that swung in his life in his mind, Sublette's held level
way, no undeserved lunge in his kind of gaze.

What he kept may fit a box put carelessly away,
but he heard some string that sang the wilderness,
monuments that pledge the rock they come from,
statues that regret their edge—and it all goes on.
Surveillance—his assignment—brings him back to us;
our work is to forget in time what if remembered might block
that great requirement which waits on its wide wings: the
wilderness. That man—fugitive from speed, antagonist of
      greatness—
comes here quietly still lost, trying to tell us what he means.

Carols Back Then: 1935

Clouds on the hills. I hear a throat voice,
chiming like Ella's from that quicksand year
soon to be gone if I do not recall
the cold and the carols that rang Christmas there.

Walls are closing round that corner scene,
the street turning to iron where we sang like a bell,
and even our classmates are shrugging away.
I stand on the curb and remember it all—

That song, the star that came near and stayed,
the hulking town we walked through that night.
I can turn to it, being true to the sign,
quietly insisting with all of my life,

That life those around me now can't know.
Ella, our town is all filling with snow!

Some Autumn Characters

I

Rain finds lost beach toys, on
open autumn days displays them
to stare through their sky window
while uninhabited islands hear crisp Rain
come toward them, their caretaker all winter
everywhere in the woods trying
to fasten down the leaves.

II

Cold, a character I used to know
in Wyoming, raps every night
at doors of lonely farms, moans
all night around the barn, and cracks
his knuckles late, late,
at the bedroom window.

III

And One Afternoon each year
is yours. It stands again
across a certain field and is the same—
a day no year can hold, but always
warm, paused in the light, looking
back and forward, where everything counts
and every bush, tree, field, or
friend will always wave.

The Girl Engaged to the Boy Who Died

A part of the wind goes around her face,
and a part still leans where the old wind
came past the radiator cap, and held
the town gently for inspection, for
years, against the cracked windshield.

A part of the room around her chair
holds like that rock at the waterfall
where floods in the park learned
the spring rules; now the trained world,
terrifying, for years, does not
come in to disturb her hair.

A part of her eye waits for a figure
that spun close in the breath she blew
at the birthday candles, and the smoke
for years wandered into corners and waited
while packages crackled in impatient hands.

And the whole sky sprang onto her blue
umbrella she held over her head when she
ran home alone, after graduation, and saw
the yard and the dingy door of her house,
and the weeds in the drive, for years.

Strangers

Brown in the snow, a car with a heater
in it searches country roads all yesterday afternoon
for our farm. At crossroads the car stops
and over the map the two people bend.
They love how the roads go on, how the heater
hums. They are so happy they can be
lost forever that afternoon.

They will probably live.
They may die. The roads go on. On the
checkered map they find themselves, and their
car is enough audience, their eyes enough
to know. If the state breaks off they will
burrow at the edge, or fall. I thought of
them yesterday, and last night sang by the
fire, thinking of them.

They are something of us, but I think better,
lost back there in our old brown car.

The Preacher at the Corner

He talked like an old gun killing buffalo,
and in what he said a giant was trying to get out;
so I listened—breathing, harkening, hearing his foghorn,
learning; for the way I found him is the way I like:
to wander because I know the road,
and find stray things, wherever they come from.

He wasn't confident: "Many a time it's bad," he said;
"I've wanted to find a hole and pull the hole
in after me." I knew that kind of dark
a radio feels, fading, or what now and then rises
toward fear in sleep: this was a man I sought, I knew—
such a target shoots out what it is at me.

Into a pass one snowy night this man
had gone among the mountains like a mild wide sound
hunting a particular way to be lost, but he came out
on a spur and knew exactly which way north was:
"And that is exactly the trouble with you," he said.
He was looking at me: "That is exactly the trouble with you."

True, I've committed innumerable sacred crimes
and followed secret paths patrolled by ivy. Unavoidable
hills have made me stern, determined not to be wavery;
so I located this man, sure enough, considerably south.
But had he glimpsed a wonderful, possible confusion?—
a strange kind of turn in the path, a kind of ivy?

The Gift

The writer's home he salvages from little pieces
along the roads, from distinctions he remembers,
from what by chance he sees—his grabbed heritage;
and from people fading from his road, from history.
He reaches out far, being a desperate man;
he comprehends by fistfuls with both hands.
But what can bring in enough to save the tame
or be home for them who even with roofs are shelterless?

We give them scenes like this:
a tree that blooms in a gale, a stone
the gale can't move, a breath song
against the pane from outside,
breathing, "Some day, tame (therefore lost) men, the wild
will come over the highest wall, waving
its banner voice, beating its gifted fist:
Begin again, you tame ones; listen—the roads
      are your home again."

Return to Single-Shot

(The John Day Country)

People who come back refuse to touch
what has been theirs, and in their speech
they give the words a twist, a foreign sound.
Cautiously they walk, wanting all they find
this time to be something else, for someone else.
Then each comes to a stop before the house
longest his, and in his perfect speech
repeats: "This is my house, and I am
still myself." And that restarts the town.

Their fingers find again the grain of wood;
they memorize the promise of the land:
what curves reliably comes back right;
to a fence, responsibility is not obsolete.
One aims a single-shot and hears the muffled past
interject that old, flat, simple sound—
the name of Daniel Boone's psychiatrist.

Remember—

The little towns day found
flowing down streets held still,
and the quiet way we lay there then,
waking?

That sheep town, say, in Nevada
where bells woke us in the dark
and we followed the ditch to a willow—
one, green?

That was almost, through quiet, the time:
the world stilled for dawn;
that instant belonged to the world.
We were there.

Coming back was toward strong light;
the town lay. Nothing was new;
still, the horizon gained something
more than color.

Out there beyond grasp was the air,
and beyond the air was a touch
any morning could bring us—
any morning.

Behind the Falls

First the falls, then the cave:
then sheets of sound around us fell
while earth fled inward, where we went.
We traced it back, cigarette lighter high—
lost the roof, then the wall,
found abruptly in that space
only the flame and ourselves,
and heard the curtain like the earth
go down, so still it made the lighter
dim that led us on under the hill.

We stopped, afraid—lost
if ever that flame went out—
and surfaced in each other's eyes,
two real people suddenly
more immediate in the dark
than in the sun we'd ever be.
When men and women meet that way
the curtain of the earth descends, and they
find how faint the light has been, how far
mere honesty or justice is from all they need.

Montana Eclogue

After the fall drive, the last
horseman humps down the trail south;
High Valley turns into a remote, still cathedral.
Stone Creek in its low bank turns calmly
through the trampled meadow. The one scouting
thunderhead above Long Top hangs to watch,
ready for its reinforcement due in October.

Logue, the man who always closes down the camp,
is left all alone at Clear Lake, where
he is leisurely but busy, pausing to glance across
the water toward Winter Peak. The bunkhouse
will be boarded up, the cookshack barricaded
against bears, the corral gates lashed shut.
Whatever winter needs, it will have to find
for itself, all the slow months the wind owns.

From that shore below the mountain the water
darkens; the whole surface of the lake livens,
and, upward, high miles of pine tops bend where a storm
walks the country. Deeper and deeper, autumn
floods in. Nothing can hold against that current
the aspens feel. And Logue, by being there, suddenly
carries for us everything that we can load on him,
we who have stopped indoors and let our faces
forget how storms come: that lonely man works for us.

Far from where we are, air owns those ranches
our trees hardly hear of, open places
braced against cold hills. Mornings, that
news hits the leaves like rain, and we
stop everything time brings, and freeze that one,
open, great, real thing—the world's gift: day.

Up there, air like an axe chops, near timberline,
the clear-cut miles the marmots own. We
try to know, all deep, all sharp, even while
busy here, that other: gripped in a job,
aimed steady at a page, or riffled by distractions,
we break free into that world of the farthest coat—air.

We glimpse that last storm when the wolves
get the mountains back, when our homes will flicker
bright, then dull, then old; and the trees
will advance, knuckling their roots or lying in
windrows to match the years. We glimpse
a crack that begins to run down the wall,
and like a blanket over the window at night
that world is with us and those wolves are here.

III

Up there, ready to be part of what comes, the high lakes
lie in their magnificent beds; but men,
great as their heroes are, live by their deeds
only as a pin of shadow in a cavern their thought
gets lost in. We pause; we stand where

we are meant to be, waver as foolish as
we are, tell our lies with all the beautiful grace
an animal has when it runs—

*Citizen, step back from the fire and let night
have your head: suddenly you more than hear
what is true so abruptly that God is cold:—
winter is here. What no one saw, has
come. Then everything the sun approved could
really fail? Shed from your back, the years
fall one by one, and nothing that comes
will be your fault. You breathe a few breaths
free at the thought: things can come so great
that your part is too small to count,
if winter can come.*

Logue brings us all that. Earth took
the old saints, who battered their hearts,
met arrows, or died by the germs God sent;
but Logue, by being alone and occurring to us,
carries us forward a little,
and on his way out for the year will
stand by the shore and see winter in,
the great, repeated lesson every year.

A storm bends by that shore and
one flake at a time teaches grace,
even to stone.

A Story

After they passed I climbed
out of my hole and sat
in the sun again. Loose rocks
all around make it safe—I can
hear anyone moving. It often
troubles me to think how others
dare live where stealth is possible,
and how they can feel safe, considering
all the narrow places,
without whiskers.

Anyway, those climbers were a puzzle—
above where I live nothing lives.
And they never came down. There is no
other way. The way it is,
they crawl far before they die.
I make my hole the deepest one
this high on the mountainside.

A Memorial Day

Said a blind fish loved that lake—
big one, doggo at the deepest place,
whiskered with scorn at any lure or bait.
Hugo said this, leading us
the road he chose years ago, to Price's Lake,
a stout authority.

He remembered this turn, that,
a rock, the way the road asked
"Where? Where?"
I watched his face swept by cat's-paws
when we found the camp tumbledown,
and back of cabins drunken Chryslers,
Hudsons even—old elephants—fallen
on alder swords through their ribs.

When winter strikes, that camp sinks
till spring, and every year
the moss gains and willows cringe
more. Coming out, our car, strong
under its hood, growled where those
old cars gasped—"Those heroes,"
Hugo said, with respect:
"I don't much go for chrome."

Quiet Town

Here in our cloud we talk
baking powder. Our yeast feet
make tracks that fill up with fog.
Tongue like a sponge, we describe
the air that we eat—how it has its own
lungs, inhales many a stranger.

Our stories have executives who flash
ornamental knives. Their children use them
afternoons to toast marshmallows.
Technicians in suicide plan courses
in high school for as long as it takes.

For our gestures, feathers are emphatic
enough; a snowflake smashes through
revealed rock. Our town balances,
and we have a railroad. Pitiful bandits
who storm the bank are led away,
their dreamy guns kicked into the gutter
by kids coming out of the movie.

No one is allowed to cross our lake at night.
Every Christmas we forget by selective remembering.
Overhead planes mutter our fear
and are dangerous, are bombs exploding
a long time, carrying bombs elsewhere to explode.

A Letter

DEAR GOVERNOR:

Rather than advise you this time or complain
I will report on one of our little towns
where I stopped last week at evening.
This town has no needs. Not one person stirred
by the three lights on Main Street. It lay
so mild and lost that I wanted you to know
how some part of your trust appears, too far
or too dim to demand or be afraid.
Now I let it all go back into its mist from
the silent river. Maybe no one will
report it to you any more.

You could think of that place annually
on this date, for reassurance—a place where we
have done no wrong. For these days to find out
what to forgive one must listen and watch:
even our friends draft us like vampires, and it is
the non-localized hurts that do the damage.
We have to forgive carefully those demands
for little helps, those unhappy acquaintances.
We must manage the ultimate necessary withdrawal
somehow, sometimes let the atoms swirl by.

So, this time, please keep on being the way
you are, and think of that town. A locust tree
put its fronds, by the way, quietly into the
streetlight; repeated breaths of river wind
came up-canyon. Let that—the nothing, the no one,
the calm night—often recur to you.

Sincerely,
A Friend

Flowers at an Airport

Part of the time sun, part of
the time shade, a limousine slides
the airport drive; the driver
gets out and stands by the curb: sun.
When they look back at our day and
ask their charts, they'll say
there never was such a time.

This is the Governor's man, to
take the Governor home. What picks
us off is time: Martin Luther
King, soldiers on patrol, kids
protected at home, the young,
the old, Lurleen.

It is a quiet day. The time is
anyone's clock—seconds like
pomegranate seeds. The man
looks over the day. Outside
what anyone knows, grackles
make a sound that imitates reeds;
their wings hover this air
that spills across the field.

This is our time. We stand
inside a curve, inside long lines
that make a more secret curve.
We hear wind through the grass.
Shadows that live in these roses fall
through thorns and become
shares in what lasts and lasts.

Texas —

Wide, no limit, the whole
state an airport, a continent
marbles could roll across; and
they say when the fist of the sun
hammers it, the natives love it,
feel they would die if moved. They
have struggled to stay, and have
won, a catastrophe. Now they deserve it—
a cruel thing to say. But true.

But wide. I came on the Sweetwater
once. It was evening, and the doves
insisted they could redeem all the
universe. Never after that could I
deny a link with Texas. A farmer
strikes oil, and stuffs his mattress
with money, like excelsior. At a
space lab they look around and think,
"Might as well try for the moon."

And they get there. Long ago
the rest of the country joined their state
and thus became, really, a part of Mexico—
why contend? Joining is better, and is done
many ways, even if politicians have limits.
I say join the state, and Mexico, and the
politicians. Beyond irony is the hard country
no one can misjudge, where we survive
our indulgences and mean just the earth again—

Texas

A Sound from the Earth

Somewhere, I think in Dakota,
they found the leg bones—just the
big leg bones—of several hundred
buffalo, in a gravel pit.

Near there, a hole in a cliff
has been hollowed so that
the prevailing wind
thrums a note so low and persistent
that bowls of water placed in that
cave will tremble to foam.

The grandfather of Crazy Horse
lived there, they say, at the last,
and his voice like the thrum of the hills
made winter come as he sang, "Boy,
where was your buffalo medicine?
I say you were not brave enough, Boy.
I say Crazy Horse was too cautious."

Then the sound he cried out for his grandson
made that thin Agency soup that they
put before him tremble. The whole
earthen bowl churned into foam.

Garden City

That town, those days, composed grand
arching pictures down by the river.
A cloud or a girl strayed by. Any storm
was temporary. Those hills to the south
rush into the lens, emboss the world;
and I can see so well that the hawks grow
pin feathers. Our class picnic
blossoms in ribbons and watermelon.

Sophomores of that year, you innocent swimmers
dissolved hundreds of times in my prayers:
the world we studied has taken us; it
opened its afternoons deep as a pond. But sometimes
Main Street at midnight flashes its fin,
or for a moment, over our days, over such
indignities as time gave us all for our share,
the monstrous blue fender of Stocky's old Hudson
reels down the white line toward home.

Memorials of a Tour Around Mt. Hood

I

At a Pioneer Cemetery

Both sides fought stillness
but stillness came:
flintlock, war cry—
now no name.

Dust holds them; restful
grass grows high:
together they grapple
the real enemy.

Overhead, fighting to break the sky,
planes trace our permanence today:
they can't go fast enough
not to go away.

II

The Cage at the Filling Station

In the turn of neck a wolverine offered
over one shoulder for his lost freedom, the world said,
Smoke ought to have a home.

People were talking; the wolverine
listened clear back to his tail. His body said,
Remember homeless ones.

39

These discontinuous gestures resting
their paws on a wall follow the thoughtful
who turn, alerted for an instant:

Smoke really ought to have a home.

III

Camping at Lost Lake

Earth at large in constellations
wafts all night our fire; and we
through the still hours feel morning
coming nearer stealthily.

Night birds flit. Darkness
takes them. Forest gulfs them all.
Our stranger eyes look for those birds
but lose them where the trees go tall.

Of course our call can't stop a bird
among those tree trunks fern has found:
our hands go out to say good-bye
as unassertive as a frond.

Among these trees till morning comes
we sleep, and dream thunders of fern
alerting space by the way they wait,
eloquent of light's return.

IV

And That Picnic at Zigzag

Tea at a campfire,
talk under the wind—
that was minimum living, Friend.

"Woe!" the wind cried;
"Hey!"—the light spied
what in the underbrush the chickadees did.

Well, we're older.
And the woods are colder.
But that was good tea, Friend.

Stories from Kansas

Little bunches of
grass pretend they are bushes
that never will bow.
    They bow.

Carelessly the earth
escapes, loping out from the
timid little towns
    toward Colorado.

Which of the horses
we passed yesterday whinnied
all night in my dreams?
    I want that one.

Things That Happen

Sometimes before great events a person will try,
disguised, at his best, not to be a clown:
he feels, "A great event is coming, bow down."
And I, always looking for something anyway,
always bow down.

Once, later than dawn but early,
before the lines of the calendar fell,
one of those events turned an unseen corner
and came near, near, sounding before it
something the opposite from a leper's bell.

We were back of three mountains called
"Sisters" along the Green Lakes trail
and had crossed a ridge when that
one little puff of air touched us,
hardly felt at all.

That was the greatest event that day;
it righted all wrong.
I remember it, the way the dust moved there.
Something had come out of the ground
and moved calmly along.

No one was ahead of us, no one
in all that moon-like land.
Oh, I thought, how hard the world has tried
with its wind, its miles, its blundering
stumbling days, again and again, to find my hand.

What I Heard Whispered at the Edge of Liberal, Kansas

Air waits for us
after we fall. It comes
perfectly together, just as a lake
does, in its every share giving
the fish paths as long
as they last. For us,
air contains all. After
we fall it waits. At the last
it is frantic with its hands
but cannot find us.
Was it a friend? Now,
too late, we think it was.

That's why we became grass.

On Don Quixote's Horse

Loose reins, the pony finds
easy trails, obvious valleys
that the grass found like birdseed,

Where thinking high we thought
hero grass around rocks
where the highest pony couldn't live.

More than valleys could be,
and air the air dreams, ponies that find other
than possible trails, thoughts like birdseed.

Walk like stilts, thought, then;
or snakelike bend, run, stand:
I call you Phantom, thought—

Trained not to be trained.

Christianite

This new kind of metal will not suffer:
it either holds or bends.
Under stress it acts like a bar, or a hinge.

This metal possesses a lucky way,
always to respond by endurance, or
an eager collapse, and forget.

(The time between the loss and the end
costs all the wear: earlier,
you win; after, you start again.)

The new metal is never in-between.
You think with it, make models,
save it for when you retire.

The impulsive cannot understand it.
Only something romantic or brittle
belongs in their hands.

Vacation Trip

The loudest sound in our car
was Mother being glum:

    Little chiding valves
    a surge of detergent oil
    all that deep chaos
    the relentless accurate fire
    the drive shaft wild to arrive

And tugging along behind in its great big
balloon,
that looming piece of her mind:

"I wish I hadn't come."

Like a Little Stone

Like a little stone, feel the shadow of the great earth;
let distance pierce you till you cling to trees.
That the world may be all the same,
close your eyes till everything is,
     and the farthest sand can vote.

Making the world be big by hunting its opposite,
go out gleaning for lost lions
that are terrified by valleys of still lambs,
for hummingbirds that dream before each wingbeat,
     for the mole that met the sun.

If time won't let a thing happen, hurry there,
to the little end of the cone that darkness bends.
Any place where you turn but might have gone on,
all possibilities need you there.
     The centers of stones need your prayers.

Note

straw, feathers, dust—
little things

but if they all go one way,
that's the way the wind goes.

Space Country

As usual the highest birds first
caught it, a slow roll even the air
hardly felt; then the thick gold haze
that many filters of eyes found
fell deep in the desert country. Wells filled
and rocks—pooled in their own shadows—
lay at ease. People did not know
why they stood up and walked, and
waited by windows or doors, or leaned
by fences to look at far scenes.
The surface of all weathered wood relaxed;
even gravel and cactus appeared soft.

The world had passed something in space
and was alone again. Sunset came on.
People lay down, and the birds forgot
as they sleepily clucked and slept, close
on boughs, as well hidden as could be
in the air again clear, sharp, and cold.

The Climb

One campfire higher every year
we hunt the height that made the wild men happy;
collecting all the wood we can
we huddle by the fire and sing
"Creeping through the Needle's Eye."

Unless old knots can rouse the flame
through swirls and melt the snow that falls,
unless the cold can draw us higher
to learn by steeper flame how rich we are,
then we may starve: it's climb-or-famine time.

An Epiphany

You thinkers, prisoners of what will work:
a dog ran by me in the street one night,
its path met by its feet in quick unthought,
and I stopped in a sudden Christmas, purposeless,
a miracle without a proof, soon lost.

But I still call, "Here, Other, Other," in the dark.

Brevities

A Speech to the Birds:
  Sparrows, I'm lucky, too.

The Neighbor Who Came to Borrow Some Bread:
  In the clutter of the workbench I find
  my cup, the coffee just cool enough to drink.

Oedipus:
  At first he won so well he lost;
  then he lost so well he won.

August:
  Summer turns from is to was—
  acres of Queen Anne's lace.

The Rock on the Summit:
  Rain told it for years,
  and it has come to believe.

Humanities Lecture

Aristotle was a little man with
eyes like a lizard, and he found a streak
down the midst of things, a smooth place for his feet
much more important than the carved handles
on the coffins of the great.

He said you should put your hand out
at the time and place of need:
strength matters little, he said,
nor even speed.

His pupil, a king's son, died
at an early age. That Aristotle spoke of him
it is impossible to find—the youth was
notorious, a conqueror, a kid with a gang,
but even this Aristotle didn't ever say.

Around the farthest forest and along
all the bed of the sea, Aristotle studied
immediate, local ways. Many of which
were wrong. So he studied poetry.
There, in pity and fear, he found Man.

Many thinkers today, who stand low and grin,
have little use for anger or power, its palace
or its prison—
but quite a bit for that little man
with eyes like a lizard.

In Fur

They hurt no one. They rove the North.
Owning the wilderness, they're not lost.
They couple in joy; in fear, they run.
Old, their lives move still the same—
all a pattern across the land,
one step, one breath, one. . . .

Winter bundles them close; their fur
bunches together in friendly storms.
Everything cold can teach, they learn.
They stand together. The future comes.

Evening News

That one great window puts forth
its own scene, the whole world
alive in glass. In it a war happens,
only an eighth of an inch thick.
Some of our friends have leaped
through, disappeared, become unknown
voices and rumors of crowds.

In our thick house, every evening
I turn from that world,
and room by room I walk, to
enjoy space. At the sink I start
a faucet; water from far is
immediate on my hand. I open our
door, to check where we live.
In the yard I pray birds,
wind, unscheduled grass,
that they please help to make
everything go deep again.

Religion Back Home

1) When God's parachute failed,
   about the spring of 1945,
   the sky in Texas jerked open
   and we all sailed easily
   into this new strange harness on the stars.

2) The minister smoked,
   and he drank,
   and there was that woman in the choir,
   but what really finished him—
   he wore spats.

3) A Short Review of *Samson Agonistes*
       Written for Miss Arrington's Class
         in Liberal High School

   Our Father Who art in Heaven
   can lick their Father Who art in Heaven.

4) When my little brother chanted,
   "In 1492 Jesus crossed the ocean blue,"
   Mother said, "Bob, you mean
   Columbus crossed the ocean blue."
   And he said, "I always did get
   them two guys mixed up."

How I Escaped

A sign said "How to Be Wild—
the Lessons Are Free,"
so I edged past, bolted inside
carefully,
where the edge of a jaguar
roved beyond bars
and narrowed the room. Its head,
one eye at a time,
sewed the tent to the stars; and the cage
ballooned when he turned.

Mid-stride, I froze and stared
past enemies
that fell in droves down aisles
of my memories.
My bones—wild flowers—burned
at whatever I'd lost,
but my enemies burned up too
in that holocaust;
and I strode on, caged from them
in disregard,
swerving, momently aimed,
like a jaguar.

Though calm now, made to forgive
by bars between,
still fitted in those paw gloves
I walk what I mean.

Mornings

1

Quiet,
rested, the brain begins to burn
and glow like a coal in the dark,
early—four in the morning, cold, with
frost on the lawn. The brain feels
the two directions of window, and as if
· holding a taper, follows the hall
that leads to the living room and silver
space; lets the town come close, the chains
of lights turned off, and purposeless feet
of chairs sprawled; lets it all rise and
subside, and the brain pulses larger
than the ordinary horizon, but deliberately
less than it wants to go. All benevolence,
the brain with its insistent little call
summons wraiths and mist layers near
from fields: the world arising and streaming
through the house, soundless, pitifully
elongated, inevitable, for review, like breathing,
quiet.

2

Waiting
in the town that flows for the brain, charmed,
weak as distance, no one can move or belong
till the brain finds them and says, "Live!"
There's one too far, the phantom beyond the brain
each day that can't hear the kindest call

(and kindness is volume in the brain's room)—
the stranger with the sudden face, of
erased body, who floats into my dream
again. Down the storm our lack of storm
implies I hear the lambs cry, every one
lost and myself lost by where I made our
home. I feel a wind inside my hand.
By a lack that our life knows, life owns its greatness:
we are led one thing at a time through gain
to that pure gain—all that we lose. Stranger,
we are blind dancers in two different rooms;
we hear the music both heard long ago: wherever
you dance, that music finds you. When you turn,
I turn. Somewhere, whatever way you move
is ours; here, I keep our place,
repeat our turns, paced by my pulse,
waiting.

3

Lowly,
I listen as fur hears the air, and by will
I think one thing at a time while the world,
complete, turns—the farm where the wheat
votes, where they have already prayed the last day;
the glass of the ocean watching the storm;
all the extreme places; and I stand at the
prow of our house, an eye (for iris the attic window),
I gaze, and see so well my listening toes blur
on the rug and realize all the way to the island
of afternoon. My hands have given their gift,
then themselves. Can't the world see humility—my
trance, my face, the sober and steady spokes of my
bicycle? Many drive in piety and for the faith

an old car. Bishops in garages care, and presbyters
at the bank judge us—all that our shoes
and their crossed laces confess; angels behind
the counter inquire the name and send it up
the dizzying tube, and listen to the building
hum our estimation. Year by year the leaves
will come again, the suspicious grass, and the air
ever more tentative over the walls one color
at a time, fish of less than water, of evening;
shadows come and the bells get ready
before they sound, one part of a hum, like my self,
lowly.

4

Light
comes inside the brain. It is early;
in the attic I hear the wind lie down.
"Stay!" I call, as we tell the dog. Sudden as
the telephone, day says, "I am here!" And
in that clear light the brain comes home, lost
from all it wandered in, unable to be
sure for questioners, caught again by needs,
reduced to its trouble with my tongue.
The frank sycamore is at the window;
dark trails sink and go backward;
the sun comes over the world, aiming
the trees at the day, hill by hill.
Light.

Spectator

Treat the world as if it really existed.
Feel in the cold what hoods a mountain—
it is not your own cold, but the world's.
Distribute for the multitude this local discovery.

In flaws of wind in the beleaguered forest
where beaver eat their aspen food
hear every moved branch as the first breath of winter;
your window tree spells the same gray sky.

Make the moment go rich in your stammering,
the grape already on the tongue,
the words thought and old before they are said—
you can have time surrounded.

There is always a place like Now to be found:
at the edge of some Utah has to be some clay valley,
and you a placid witness of dinosaur bones.
You are foreign, part of some slow explosion.

Any Time

Vacation? Well, our children took our love apart:
"Why do you hold Daddy's hand?" "Susy's mother
doesn't have gray in her hair." And scenes crushed
our wonder—Sun Valley, Sawtooths, those reaches
of the Inland Passage, while the children took our
simple love apart.

(Children, how many colors does the light have?
Remember the wide shafts of sunlight, roads
through the trees, how light examines the road hour
by hour? It is all various, no simple on-off colors.
And love does not come riding west through the
trees to find you.)

"Daddy, tell me your best secret." (I have woven
a parachute out of everything broken; my scars
are my shield; and I jump, daylight or dark,
into any country, where as I descend I turn
native and stumble into terribly human speech
and wince recognition.)

"When you get old, how do you know what to do?"
(Waves will quiet, wind lull; and in that
instant I will have all the time in the world;
something deeper than birthdays will tell me all I need.)
"But will you do right?" (Children, children,
oh see that waterfall.)

Folk Song

First no sound, then you hear it—
so *Sally*, so *Tom*:
it is the past, its wisdom,
quick in the head again.

Back then when the moon climbed home
and someone began the song,
we were a people together
alive in the bush again.

Now, puzzle it with notes for a while,
shake it over the land:
this is your country, broken,
and broken and broken again.

Sing it together till you hold it—
all Sally, all Tom:
make our time, its promise,
come true in the air again.

Believing What I Know

A lake on the map of Canada
may forget in the snow—
in the spring be gone.

Imagine the flower-eyes
nodding a little breeze,
looking at the land where the lake was.

Many things that were true
disappeared, grew up in grass,
and now hide from flowers that stare.

I learn from the land. Some day
like a field I may take the next thing
so well that whatever is will be me.

Where We Are

Much travel moves mountains large
in your eyes—and then inside,
where those mountains climb the Everest
of all thought—tomorrows and maybes—
where expeditions often get lost.

Slow travel moves mountains best—
they pivot with dignity and bow
after you pass; they accompany
caravans for days, now and then
attacking, are driven back with snow.

We live in that cold range now
where the temporary earth tries
for something greater, with the keen air's aid,
and more, where the world perishes day
by day in the tall winter beyond any range.

In the Old Days

The wide field that was the rest of the world
came forward at evening, lowered
beyond our window shades; and Mother
spoke from her corner, about the wide field:

How someone whose eyes held another century
brought shadows of strange animals
over the mountains, and they were tethered
at night in little groups in the wide field,

And their eyes like wandering sparks
made constellations against the trees;
and how, many skies later, my father left
those animals and brought Mother news of the wide field.

Some time, some sunset, our window, she said,
would find itself again with a line of shadows
and the strange call would surround our house
and carry us away through the wide field.

Then Mother sang. But we listened, beyond:
we knew that the night she had put into a story was real.

Tragic Song

All still when summer is over
stand shocks in the field,
nothing left to whisper,
not even good-bye, to the wind.

After summer was over
we knew winter would come:
we knew silence would wait,
tall, patient, calm.

And that cold this winter gray wolves
deep in the North would cry
how summer that whispered all of us
at last whispers away.

At Our House

Home late, one lamp turned low,
crumpled pillow on the couch,
wet dishes in the sink (late snack),
in every child's room the checked,
slow, sure breath—

Suddenly in this doorway where I stand
in this house I see this place again,
this time the night as quiet, the house
as well secured, all breath but mine borne
gently on the air—

And where I stand, no one.

Deerslayer's Campfire Talk

At thousands of places on any
mountain, exact rock faces lean
a strong-corner slant, balanced:
the whole country stays by such dependable
sets and shoulders—which endure unnoted.
　　Bend after bend the river washes
its hands, never neglecting to kiss
every drop to every other—but that
is a small thing, not important.
　　Tribes, or any traveling people,
will have some who stoke the fire
or carry the needed supplies—but
they take few great positions; hardly
anyone cares about them.

Wherever I go they quote people
who talk too much, the ones who
do not care, just so they take the center
and call the plans.
　　When I see these things, a part of my
mind goes quiet, and by a little turn
of my eyes I favor what helps, and ordinary
men, and that dim arch above us we seldom
regard, and—under us—the silent,
unnoted clasp of the rock.

In Fog

In fog a tree steps back.

Once gone, it joins those hordes
blizzards rage for over tundra.

With new respect I tell
my dreams to grant all claims;

Lavishly, my eyes close between
what they saw and that far flood

Inside: the universe that happens
deep and steadily.

Time

The years to come (empty boxcars
waiting on a siding while someone forgets
and the tall grass tickles their bellies)
will sometime stay, rusted still;
and a little boy who clambers up,
saved by his bare feet, will run
along the top, jump to the last car,
and gaze down at the end into that river
near every town.
                    Once when I was a boy
I took that kind of walk,
beyond the last houses, out where the grass
lived, then the tired siding where trains whistled.
The river was choked with old Chevies and Fords.
And that was the day the world ended.

Allegiances

It is time for all the heroes to go home
if they have any, time for all of us common ones
to locate ourselves by the real things
we live by.

Far to the north, or indeed in any direction,
strange mountains and creatures have always lurked—
elves, goblins, trolls, and spiders:—we
encounter them in dread and wonder,

But once we have tasted far streams, touched the gold,
found some limit beyond the waterfall,
a season changes, and we come back, changed
but safe, quiet, grateful.

Suppose an insane wind holds all the hills
while strange beliefs whine at the traveler's ears,
we ordinary beings can cling to the earth and love
where we are, sturdy for common things.

These Days

Hurt people crawl as if they
suddenly love each part of themselves
again, after years of neglect,
as if the next place they might find
could bring a new sun in its hand,
or a mist they could separate and follow.

As if any time a bird might call and it
will be day, or from a ditch a cousin
or a lover will sing, hurt people
curiously turn their heads,
as if their duty, in a democracy, if
we are to have peace, is quickly
to crawl away over the horizon.

Earth Dweller

It was all the clods at once become
precious; it was the barn, and the shed,
and the windmill, my hands, the crack
Arlie made in the axe handle: oh, let me stay
here humbly, forgotten, to rejoice in it all;
let the sun casually rise and set.
If I have not found the right place,
teach me; for, somewhere inside, the clods are
vaulted mansions, lines through the barn sing
for the saints forever, the shed and windmill
rear so glorious the sun shudders like a gong.

Now I know why people worship, carry around
magic emblems, wake up talking dreams
they teach to their children: the world speaks.
The world speaks everything to us.
It is our only friend.

A Walk in the Country

To walk anywhere in the world, to live
now, to speak, to breathe a harmless
breath: what snowflake, even, may try
today so calm a life,
so mild a death?

Out in the country once,
walking the hollow night,
I felt a burden of silver come:
my back had caught moonlight
pouring through the trees like money.

That walk was late, though.
Late, I gently came into town,
and a terrible thing had happened:
the world, wide, unbearably bright,
had leaped on me. I carried mountains.

Though there was much I knew, though
kind people turned away,
I walked there ashamed—
into that still picture
to bring my fear and pain.

By dawn I felt all right;
my hair was covered with dew;
the light was bearable; the air
came still and cool.
And God had come back there
to carry the world again.

Since then, while over the world
the wind appeals events,
and people contend like fools,
like a stubborn tumbleweed I hold,
hold where I live, and look into every face:

Oh friends, where can one find a partner
for the long dance over the fields?

So Long

At least at night, a streetlight
is better than a star.
And better good shoes on a
long walk, than a good friend.

Often in winter with my old
cap I slip away into the gloom
like a happy fish, at home
with all I touch, at the level of love.

No one can surface till far,
far on, and all that we'll have
to love may be what's near
in the cold, even then.

About the Author

WILLIAM STAFFORD was born in Hutchinson, Kansas, in 1914, and studied at the University of Kansas and the University of Iowa, where he received his doctorate. In his time he has been a laborer in sugar-beet fields, an oil refinery and the U.S. Forest Service, has worked for the Church of the Brethren and for Church World Service, and taught in high schools and in colleges in Kansas, Iowa, California, Indiana, and Oregon. He has been on the faculty of Lewis and Clark College in Portland, Oregon, since 1948, where he is now Professor of English.

Mr. Stafford is the author of three earlier books of poetry, *West of Your City* (1960), *Traveling through the Dark* (published by Harper & Row in 1962 and recipient of the National Book Award for Poetry), and *The Rescued Year* (1966). His poems have appeared in many magazines and have been widely anthologized, and they have brought him honorary degrees and numerous awards. He gives frequent and welcome readings of his poetry throughout the country, from college campuses to the Library of Congress.

Mr. Stafford lives in Lake Oswego, Oregon, with his wife and their four children, all of whom are campers, bicyclers, travelers, and readers like their father.